verdant

truth serum vol. 5

First published as a collection July 2020
Content copyright © Truth Serum Press and individual authors
Edited by Matt Potter

BP#00091

All rights reserved by the authors and publisher. Except for brief excerpts used for review or scholarly purposes, no part of this book may be reproduced in any manner whatsoever without express written consent of the publisher or the author/s.

Truth Serum Press
32 Meredith Street
Sefton Park SA 5083
Australia

Email: truthserumpress@live.com.au
Website: https://truthserumpress.net/
Store: https://truthserumpress.net/catalogue/

Original front cover image copyright © Jeon Sang-O
Cover design copyright © Matt Potter

ISBN: 978-1-922427-04-5

Also available as an eBook
ISBN: 978-1-922427-05-2

A note on differences in punctuation and spelling:
Truth Serum Press proudly features writers from all over the English-speaking world. Some speak and write English as their first language, while for others, it's their second or third or even fourth language. Naturally, across all versions of English, there are differences in punctuation and spelling, and even in meaning. These differences are reflected in the work *Truth Serum Press* publishes, and they account for any differences in punctuation, spelling and meaning found within these pages.

Truth Serum Press is a member of the
Bequem Publishing collective
http://www.bequempublishing.com/

verdant

(vɜːʳdənt)

ADJECTIVE

If you describe a place as verdant, you mean that it is covered with green grass, trees, and plants.

[literary]

...a small verdant garden with a view out over Paris.

from **Collins Online English Dictionary**

https://www.collinsdictionary.com/dictionary/english/

There was a verdant pasture somewhere
Whose land was the very picture of beauty

from ***A Cow and a Goat***
by Allama Muhammad Iqbal

· Joseph ALLISON · David ATKINSON · Shawn AVENINGO-SANDERS · Linda BARRETT · Dev BERGER · Michael BERTON · Henry BLADON · Paula BONNELL · John BOST · Howard BROWN · William BUTLER · Laurie BYRO · Ann CEFOLA · Guy CHAMBERS · Yael CHANOFF · Chuka Susan CHESNEY · Jan CHRONISTER · Dave CLARK · Linda M. CRATE · Luciana CROCI · Mary DAURIO · Karen DAVIDSON · John DAVIS · Ruth Z. DEMING · Joanie DiMARTINO · Miriam DRORI · Bina Sarkar ELLIAS · PM FLYNN · Myrna GARANIS · Christian GARDUNO · Declan GERAGHTY · Ken GOSSE · John GREY · Jan HAAG · Michael HALL · Ryn HOLMES · Matthew HORSFALL · Mark HUDSON · Sheena HUSSAIN · Tim JARVIS · Fiona M. JONES · Sarah Jane JUSTICE · Shannon KERNAGHAN · Norman KLEIN · Robyn LANCE · John LAUE · Ron. LAVALETTE · Christine LAW · Larry LEFKOWITZ · Cynthia LESLIE-BOLE · Mike LEWIS-BECK · Chelsea LOGAN · Chuck MADANSKY · Jan McCARTHY · Luke McDONOUGH · Deborah MELTVEDT · Karla Linn MERRIFIELD · Anna MIODUCHOWSKA · Marsha MITTMAN · Colleen MOYNE · Remngton MURPHY · Piet NIEUWLAND · Carl 'Papa' PALMER · Kathryn PAULSEN · Gary PERCESEPE · Felix PURAT · Alex ROBERTSON · Ruth Sabath ROSENTHAL · Paula RUDNICK · Ed RUZICKA · Kathryn SADAKIERKSI · Jeff SANTOSUOSSO · Gerard SARNAT · Mir-Yashar SEYEDBAGHERI · Laura Jan SHORE · Linda SIMONE · Mary TRAFFORD · Mark TULIN · Lucy TYRRELL · Patricia UNSWORTH · Jill VANCE · George WHITESTONE · Debbie WIESS · Ron WILKINS · Allan J. WILLS · Melissa WONG · Stephen WREN · Amelia Clare WRIGHT · Mantz YORKE ·

1	One of the Flock	Ron Lavalette
2	A Pair of Evergreens	Jan McCarthy
3	rather an empty cup	Linda M. Crate
4	Dark Pursuit	PM Flynn
6	Measures and Rules	Norman Klein
7	Green Card Soldier	Carl 'Papa' Palmer
8	The Obscene Green – or – I Was a Guy Who Couldn't Say No	Ken Gosse
10	St Augustine, The Destroyer	Jeff Santosuosso
12	Lust	Ryn Holmes
14	Ode to the Hills	Mir-Yashar Seyedbagheri
16	Finger Time	Chuka Susan Chesney
18	The Lord Gave Us Luscious Acres Of Greenery	Ruth Z. Deming
19	I Am a Tree	Bina Sarkar Ellias
20	how you died out in me	Gary Percesepe
22	duende	Chuck Madansky
23	Crow Feet	Sheena Hussain
24	Start	Mike Lewis-Beck
26	The Green Machine	Remington Murphy
28	Verdigris	Allan J. Wills

30	Sycamore Bower	Matthew Horsfall
31	Replace two doorknobs	John Bost
32	Camo	Cynthia Leslie-Bole
34	Shoveling Snow	Linda Barrett
35	Storm Season	Yael Chanoff
36	An Undesirable Object	Christine Law
37	The Girl With Green Eyes in the Goethe-Institut in Iéna	Felix Purat
38	Sad Rags	Patricia Unsworth
39	Prasinophobia	Henry Bladon
40	Stopping at the Green Light	Tim Jarvis
42	Grass	Sarah Jane Justice
43	Bequeath Only Tears	George Whitestone
44	Black Thumb	Amelia Clare Wright
48	street view	Lucy Tyrrell
50	At the grove	Piet Nieuwland
51	The Verdancy of Green	Ruth Sabath Rosenthal
54	An Ancient River	Mark Tulin
56	Climate Change Fears	Gerard Sarnat
57	Growth	Jan Chronister
58	Uaine	Christian Garduno

59	When We Were On the Sea	William Butler
60	Margaret's Green Man	Laurie Byro
62	Give Me the Herbivores in Life	Larry Lefkowitz
63	Weeds	Chelsea Logan
64	The Last Olive	Michael Berton
67	The Virtues of Roots	Ann Cefola
68	Coffee Good Friday Morning	Ed Ruzicka
70	Greenhorn	Marsha Mittman
71	Under Lockdown, Manchester	Mantz Yorke
72	Rhombus of Brightness	Stephen Wren
74	Willowspring	Paula Bonnell
76	The Green Boots	Mark Hudson
78	The Park	Declan Geraghty
79	An Everglades Romance	Karla Linn Merrifield
80	What You Put Me Through	John Grey
82	Green Heaven	Michael Hall
84	Voice of Autumn	John Davis
86	The Palm	Miriam Drori
87	Tunnel of Green	Howard Brown
88	Winter Morning	Anna Mioduchowska
90	Verdant Envy	Debbie Wiess

92	Long May Your Big Jib Draw	Shannon Kernaghan
94	The tangled garden	Karen Davidson
96	Pan Flash	Guy Chambers
98	How Aussie is that	Dave Clark
99	Birdbrain	Paula Rudnick
100	St Patrick's Day	Colleen Moyne
102	Finding green	Mary Trafford
104	Of ringbarked trees by moonlight	Ron Wilkins
106	Perfect	Fiona M. Jones
108	Cooking in the glut	Robyn Lance
109	A Prickly Relationship	David Atkinson
110	The Way of the Grasshopper	Luciana Croci
111	I've found the green	Jill Vance
112	Poppies	Jan Haag
115	Plague of locusts	Myrna Garanis
116	In the Next Galaxy	Laura Jan Shore
117	Training Wheels	Shawn Aveningo-Sanders
118	Hair	Luke McDonough
121	Cutting the grass	Melissa Wong
122	Vine – The *Big Island* of Hawaii	John Laue
124	Fallen Companion	Mary Daurio

125	Sans Color	Kathryn Paulsen
126	Weeds in the Wasteland	Joseph Allison
127	The Absence of Green, Spring 2020	Deborah Meltvedt
128	Green Eyes	Kathryn Sadakierski
130	Outside Her Window	Dev Berger
132	Picture This	Linda Simone
134	A Matter of Substance	Alex Robertson
136	Remarks in a Writing Studio	Joanie DiMartino

One of the Flock

Ron. Lavalette

He never really knows which curve
will hide the flock of wild turkeys
that almost every morning
struts and pecks its way across
from field to field, either
oblivious to or ignorant of traffic,
intent on only what can be
found and eaten, whatever it is
that turkeys, long before sunrise,
seek.
      All he really wants, driving
away from his bed, driving away
from anything bedlike and restful,
is another day of certainty about
anything; another reassurance
that goals can be obtained;
that, like him, the sun will rise;
that grass can indeed be greener.

A Pair of Evergreens

Jan McCarthy

In dark diluvian mud of an allotment
under a watery English summer sun
I hunker down, Eden-ed, the green snakes
of broad beans uncoiling in my hands

These are the hands of a grower dilettante,
proud nurturer of beans and radishes
and everlasting stir-fry rainbow chard,
of blancher of Brussels, stewer of summer squashes,
slicer of corpses of carrots Chantenay

I care not for the hoots of passers-by
at my elevated, rounded derrière
nor the arthritic twinges in the hinges
the which will soon be healed with tea and rest

Here I am and here I stubborn stay
an arm's length from my grafter of a husband
who has ambitious plans and sharp desire
for fragrant herbs, exotic fruits and hops

We are a well-matched pair
exchanging smiles and ouches

rather an empty cup

Linda M. Crate

the jungle of your green eyes
doesn't really haunt me much any more,
but i think it is because i have become
adept at taking other predators
down at this point;
i know not to trust every thing that moves in
the grass as an ally—

i usually love green eyes,
but i know there is a discord in yours;
a poison that encircles every
disney villain and you

so i will forever keep my distance
from any drink the universe pours of you
into my cup—

rather an empty cup than a cup of death
because i have many more dreams and universes
to make realities, and i am not the fool that embraces
every gift I'm given because some gifts are really
curses—
trojan horses carrying enemies to your door,
and i will not be slain.

Dark Pursuit

PM Flynn

Night: a car approaches from behind. Laughter
and rusty springs ride squeaky rhythms around a curve.
Headlights sweep the forest followed with a ghostly exhaust.
Red stars sneak 'round two-lane corners without staring.
The smoke drifts on the pavement as pale figures
behind the wheel disappear over and down a hill.

Sunrise: warm and cool shadows hug the edge of the highway.

Dodging Potholes: cool air under the forest rolls the median dust.
Maple leaves tumble like cards, landing on upstairs windowsills.

Dusk: midriff clouds hang over the rails of November's belted fields.
Winter is close.
Steel air rusts below a low, damp sun peering through
the blue-gray sky.
There are more colors beside the powdered road.

Orange: I've forgotten her words.

Black: leaves disappearing under a passing car.

Brown: leaves before mulching moral equivalents.

Yellow: leaves cooler to the touch than the sun's haze.

Red: leaves on fire without smoke.

Green: what remains of a day.

Tonight: the orange sin of a rising moon
hides behind trees neither full nor bare.
Leaves caught by dark, pursuing waters drift downstream.

Measures and Rules

Norman Klein

I loved her. She was my dreams come true, just plain perfect.

I can't help remembering the day she walked me into the meadow and sat me down beneath the ancient oak on the top of the hill. We watched as the dark clouds gathered, then the thunder and lightning slashing through the green leaves as it began to rain. In minutes we were love soaked. So I took off my shirt.

She chuckled as she took off her shoes, and we kissed, and I said, "Here we are at the gate. Will you have me?"

"No, not until next Saturday. That's the day we pick up our rings."

Green Card Soldier

Carl 'Papa' Palmer

seasonal migrant worker
unwed mother in Arizona
temporary work visa expires
sent back across the border

unwed mother in Arizona
allows her teen-aged son
sent back across the border
the chance to have a better life

allows her teen-aged son
now after his first eighteen years
the chance to have a better life
by staying and joining the US Army

now after his first eighteen years
he fights to become an American
by staying and joining the US Army
by becoming an American fighting man

he fights to become an American
offers his life for this country
by becoming an American fighting man
becomes an American citizen, posthumously

The Obscene Green – or – I Was a Guy Who Couldn't Say No

Ken Gosse

They said, "Try some kale;
a gourmet's holy grail,"
but my taste buds are frail
and it tasted like stale
escargot—
yes, that's snail.

It causes the tongue
of a gila to flail.
My cat's awful wail
when she sniffed it
screamed, "Fail!"
I'd rather eat mail
or that stuff in the pail
that the cooks always bail,
or blubber of whale,
warm and raw—
don't inhale!—

but I fell to the spell
of this blight of delight,
assured I'd be fine
if I tried it, despite
my compulsion for flight
from this dreaded dark knight;
then my knuckles turned white
and my throat
spasmed tight!

The last thing I saw
at the end of this plight
as I wandered ungently
into that good night:
the horizon, where dawn
would no longer burn bright,
'neath the blur of
the firmament's stars'
dimming light,
for I tried just one bite.
Now I see, in hindsight

my finis.
C'est la vie.
Lost the fight.

St Augustine, The Destroyer

Jeff Santosuosso

after "In Bloom," by Nirvana

Lush lawn lays deep to the east,
awaits the afternoon sun to the west,
grass greening in daylight,
blades extending, abundant.

St Augustine, St Augustine,
malicious runners!

Scorched Earth vines
like Gatling gunners!

Roots have been watered,
plump, clutching the soil,
firm and plush,
growing in the sod bed.

St Augustine, St Augustine,
violent greenery.
St Augustine, St Augustine,
tyrant of the scenery!

I stand on the porch,
admiring my success,
neighbors' certain envy,
a Southern satisfaction.

St Augustine, St Augustine
devours all the others!
St Augustine, St Augustine,
bystanders all smothered!

Lust

Ryn Holmes

With a soft rustle of new leaves,
an artful form twines overhead,
slowly unwinds toward Woman.
Its lispy voice dances,
oozes unctuous utterings
through dagger-teeth,
clings to her nakedness.

Parsing her naiveté,
something catches its eye.
Aha! What might this be?
Such pleasing shape and splendid color!
Suggesting the forbidden to her,
its mischief smooth Guile.

Fascinated by the creature's sinuousness,
new sensations arise – Desire.
A first look at the red object
teaches Covet. *Why not, then?*
With a wicked kiss from Temptation,
she reaches out, bites.

Gazing with Guilty fascination
upon the creature's Beauty
receding in the verduous grass,
she ponders unwelcomed Danger.
It creeps in with a twinge of Pain –
the first of monthly courses.
She recalls another Voice:

Take anything you like – with one exception.

Ode to the Hills

Mir-Yashar Seyedbagheri

the lawyer comes only once a week,
the accountant, the doctor too,
but voluptuous hillsides seduce us with
verdant shadows and curvaceous roads.
ATVs roaring and flesh-worn smiles
unfurled beneath dusk's purple sweat, shadows zigzagging
over grass and dirt, for
time is the lady who slumbers

a month a day, a year a month
and the main street curves around a hill,
stops and ends,
in between we wander among
hardware, thrift stores where we
pay it forward to the least
coffee shops darkened at four o'clock
we all find amusement at the market,

deliberating over six-packs and corn
talking about weather and the thrill of the hunt
with a smile
we go to the market and hills every day,
and surrender to homes at night,
lights flicker like melted butter,
homes snaking out from hills

rolling, up and down, up and down,
we let loose in evening's symphonies,
lavender, purple, gold,
bursting across the pines
around curvaceous roads
over rustic living rooms
which beckon us to dream, to sleep
among the pines and hills

Finger Time

Chuka Susan Chesney

He says buy a pepper
any color but green
and scallions and avocado
so I surf the website
choose a list of items
til it's time to click the
shopping cart a graphic
with no germs

I review everything I've bought
with expectancy I scan
brown rice Quaker oats
gluten-free bread hot dogs
fizzy apple cider maybe bleach?
and those veggies he wants
to toss a salad next week

Now perhaps we'll be okay

Time to get a delivery day
No delivery available
end of week nothing
then it stops no more days

Someone tells me you just have to sit
waiting with your finger poised
til suddenly there's an open spot
then you click
like a frantic clock
before anybody else who's ticking does

Even though I'm trapped at home
my ravenous finger taps the desk
for when the delivery
sentence will appear

The Lord Gave Us Luscious Acres Of Greenery

Ruth Z. Deming

Green tea I drink every morning to get my motor running
Stem of purple hyacinth narcissus I picked
while walking around the block
Pea soup cooking in the slo-cooker I bought 8 years ago
before the woman from Bellorussia closed her shop
Boyfriend Scott in his green Philadelphia Eagles sweatshirt
bringing me food, blessed food, in these trying times.
Green bananas not fit to eat, yet.
Gangrene, an obese, sugar-addicted friend, lost two precious toes.
The smell of green onions, popping up on the front lawn
I pull out a bunch like saving a drowning victim by the hair
and sniff, sniff, sniff.
A philodendron basking in sunshine
by the window in my kitchen
its mottled green leaves, silently falling each day
like tears
Winnie asked me to adopt it since she was dying
of cancer, and did, four years ago.
My dead friend's photo, Stephen Weinstein
looking over my shoulder. No idea of the
horrors we face every day by the silly name
finally become real: Covid-19.

I Am a Tree

Bina Sarkar Ellias

a tree lives inside me
its cloistered roots
anchor my
nomad mind
its gnarled trunks
hold my spine
its branches
stretch into
the hidden sky
of my ruminations
its leaves
are green words
that sing songs
of enchantment
when stirred
by the breeze
of new beginnings
that drift through
my blue veins~
its precious fruit
is plucked and peeled
for untold narratives~

a tree lives inside me.
i am a tree.

how you died out in me

Gary Percesepe

slowly,
like the last star
shivering in the
black sky

green-eyed lamps
inside me
at the point
where one says
never

down to the last
worn out
knot of breath

not there, with a
splinter
of life

in the cross of
your arms everything
fell into you

then dimmed

out of a
thousand
light years
a few
minutes
remained

to know what you
gave to me
with no idea
what you
received

duende

Chuck Madansky

That wound, a light
white binding, pointing
slightly heartward
on the first finger
from my right thumb,
the one that flicks
gypsy moth worms
from my left forearm
in this season
of green devouring.

My mother
told me not to ride
my bike so fast
and I did and clipped
my finger on the left
fin of a Chevy Impala,
chrome bloodied—
the slight smile
on my mother's mouth.

Crow Feet

Sheena Hussain

Beyond habitual quietness,
I hear the hands pass in sync with
throbbing through the left breast pocket.
Marred with a constant itch in my head,
a monastic cell reminds me I am duty bound.
Awkwardly, placing a wilting weight I grip the armchair
tracing paisley patterns with my pointer finger:
Nervously, hoping to catch a glimpse of a colony
or even a light conversation
as King Solomon had, as an elect of God.
In a flash, the northern nightingale neatly perches upon
the feeder, feet locked as if a boatswain anchor;
This specific one chooses to live greedy,
encroaching tomorrow's fill and space.
Across, lives a crow atop the chimney pot
nestling there for years, spying in on me
like a nosey neighbour gifted with Hawkeye
Snarled face with wrinkles, caws hangs over
as a shadow of death, heavily weighing me down to earth.
After preening, fading away in one flutter,
not long before you are dead.
Until then the Lord's Prayer is to be read
In the green carpet I plant my feet
I stand, still, I see something
acutely sacrilegious…

Start

Mike Lewis-Beck

Start the new day watching your waking
to the smell of cherry blossoms that wafts
through the window with wheel rolls
from the cars on a red brick road
that leads to town, to bureaus and benches.

A day starts over, its past a promise
of sun rise and night fall
over the green spring lawns
before the dawn houses that line
the promenade of ladies off to hot yoga.

The cardinal on the wire starts
in song, a *credo-credo* whistle to call
his mate, a grey eminence at the feeder
filled with corn by widow Jones,
next door and doing house with her sister.

I start at their faded faces, begin again
to wonder at the cardinal who keeps
his love warble in the face
of a cloudburst that scatters two lovebirds—
a boy and girl hand-in-hand.

They hold on tight in the wet, run
for cover under a mighty oak, laugh
off a lightning warning. The hands drop,
then not, as their minds change. Some dreams
never end—they just start over.

The Green Machine

Remngton Murphy

Why does the seed have to germinate?
Why does the root, in its impetus,
Have to push through the dirt?
Why does the trunk, defying gravity,
Thrust ever upward?
Why does it have to do this?
What gives it the right?

When it begins leafing,
When it sails upon the air,

Strong as a fortress,
Yet delicate, light as a feather,
Threatening to break,
Precarious on the wind, creaking,
Like a wooden ship of old
Fabulously laden,

When it soars,
Thriving, branching out,
When it offers up its shade,
Yielding up its fruit,

Why does the tree have to do this?
What's the point?

When the spring, for all its imperfections,
For all its starts and interruptions,
Nevertheless muddles through,
What's the big idea?

Verdigris

Allan J. Wills

Clean
Verdigris
From
Neglected levers

How much brass
Turned
How fast or slow
A lifetime?
How long
The welfare lines?

Airport
Conga dancers
Embrace
Disperse
Elsewhere— or here?

Bronzed
Beach
Belles and beaus
Complacent
Disport
Elsewhere— or here?

Bell curve
Path of fears?
Bridge of tears!
The horror!
The horror!

Tap
Wash hands
Twenty seconds
Soap water
Happy song

Mirror
Too close
A stranger
Two metres
My child
A hug

Closed
Workplaces
Borders
Doors
Keep open an inch of heart

Sycamore Bower

Matthew Horsfall

Rye grass mowed down swathes homeward
Bound in autumn sweet and dappled sleep.
Old names dream death in the shade evergreen

Of a sycamore bower. Unkempt and overgrown:
Rosemary, poppy, dandelion. Indian summer
Weeds oblivious to the pageantry of April.

The cenotaph stands alone. A stolen diamond
Worn down to old bone. The time erased names:
Pretoria, Mafeking, Paardeburg, Bloemfontein.

We cannot forget a truth we never knew.
We do not tend the shrine anymore. What remains?
A lesser war, an obedience, our youth?

Replace two doorknobs

John Bost

Replace two doorknobs ...
With cheese on a cracker
Yes, maybe a nice slice of cheddar
You know there's not too much better —
Though you do like that wool sweater
Enjoy getting a handwritten letter
Or even a picture postcard —

Remember playing in your backyard
Running around and flying up in the air
Ready for adventure way out there
Where once a week you'd mow that green lawn
And when you were done you were gone
Exploring the woods or off on your bike
You might visit with Mitch or wave to Mike
Who lived down at the bottom of the hill
And now you wonder who lives there still

There's nothing really quite like cheese on a cracker
You could replace two doorknobs and not be a slacker
Or what the heck go ahead   have some cheese on a cracker

Camo

Cynthia Leslie-Bole

we wear camouflage
drab greens and browns of jungle vines
soothing tans and creams of desert sands
combat colors for our protection
to hide from the enemy's deadly aim

we layer on the grease paint
sew leaves and grasses onto the uniform
blend with the background
peer disembodied from dense cover
with watching, swiveling eyes

but once the enemy is vanquished
we find the makeup doesn't wash off and
the mottled fabric has become our skin
the threat has receded, but we remain on high alert
ready to react should war games resume

how to find the self beneath the disguise?
first take a long soak in nonpartisan waters
floating free of judgment in transparent liquid
let the layers of concealment melt away
like dead skin sloughing off after sunburn

next, emerge raw and naked
don't succumb to the desire for cover
leave your tender parts exposed
feel the safety of wind, the solace of sun
the gentle licks of rain, the air vibrating your nerves

finally, choose new colors
flaming orange, spring green, pulsing purple
select your favorite fabrics
satin and silk, rough linen, organic cotton
try things on, feel for fit without a mirror

too long you have dressed
from threat instead of trust
bedeck your body with courage
then show yourself at last—
the battle has long been over

Shoveling Snow

Linda Barrett

Winter, that old bitch,
dumped a ton of snow
on the Eastern Seaboard
So it's me outside,
digging out my driveway
Shoveling down to the gnarled
asphalt,
Looking down into one of its
cracks,
a small rolled up green shoot
stares back at me,
signifying the verdant hope
of the coming spring.

Storm Season

Yael Chanoff

The air's so calm and cool now
Between dazed heat and dirty cold
Her kids can play in the front yard for hours
We watch them from tree stumps
And even as I rub her back
And we whisper about death
The girls fly on their swings
Jump off to play with branches
Young oak ripped up by last night's thunderstorm
Sparse leaves still green
And even as she chokes back tears
The baby walks up to her – he's walking now –
And in her arms he breathes in that sweet breeze
Stretches and says "ah."

An Undesirable Object

Christine Law

The parcel feels heavy it's a gift
From Great Aunt Joan.
What am I supposed to do with this?
Agnes shrieks.

It looks like a Green bottle with a dent
In the middle.
Why did Great Aunt Joan buy it?
Can it be passed off as modern art?

The sun shines, casting a shadow
Through the window pane,
Maybe it isn't so bad the glass shines
Bright.
So do the ashes in memory of
Great Aunt Joan.

The Girl With Green Eyes in the Goethe-Institut in Iéna

Felix Purat

Light beams with intuition
Green eyes never scary
Something pleasant to admire

Glowering with Faustian fire
Within the white, postwar room
Where no hypothermic water flows

To douse the hellish flames
We use to immolate the world
Stare after verdant stare

Sad Rags

Patricia Unsworth

I am wearing green today. Hat, coat, shoes.
Tomorrow I might wear red, but today,
today I wear green.

My head spins with envy, darkest of green.
It is in my eyes, it is in my heart.
Your betrayal bites.

The heels of my shoes sink in the long grass
blending colour almost invisible.
Matching green with green.

And it was on this grass you betrayed me.
You and she, lovers, lustful, unaware,
but I had seen you.

Today it is green to match my jealousy.
Tomorrow I shall wear red. Hat, coat, shoes.
Red to match my rage.

More colours remain to feed my revenge.
There is the funeral black. Hat, coat, shoes
to wear last of all. But soon....

Prasinophobia

Henry Bladon

For the most part, the chef likes his job.
If he were not a chef, he fancied he might be a poet.

In his kitchens, although he has banned the playing
of any opera music by Verdi, he follows in the tradition
of Picasso, Proust and Poe and is partial to a mug or two of absinthe.

He has posted a list of banned food items, which are:

Lettuce
celery
mint and
lime,
parsley
sage
rosemary and
thyme.

And peas.

Imagine how must easier his life would be
if they were all blue.

Stopping at the Green Light

Tim Jarvis

I'm the green light on your answer machine.
Flashing like a beacon.
Asking you to press play.
Waiting for you to hear my message.
Telling you…hey.
It's me.
I'm so glad you didn't pick up.
I just wanted to say something,
while it's fresh in my head.
I ran across an old picture and it took me back.
I wanted to call.
A few times.
Obviously, I didn't.
I guess I still have questions.
Do you even think about what happened?
And wonder where we'd be if it didn't?
I do.
It makes me die a little inside each time.
I still feel the pull of you now and again.
You can't just put it in a safe and throw away the key.
Was it as good as I remember?
Or worse than I thought?
Who knows?
I just wish you were more, I don't know, positive.
All I wanted was for you to see the stars shining.

But you saw nothing out there but cold, dead rocks.
Maybe it was us who were distant and dying.
You never were much of an optimist.
There were a million little battles that I was never going to win
What was it you always used to say? Love is a do-it-yourself project.
I gave and I gave, and I tried, and I tried
And you threw it away. Like a cigarette in the street.
I hate loving you.
I don't know what I'm saying
Like every voicemail I've ever left, this isn't going to plan.
I should really write things down more.
What I'm trying to say is people change. As does everything.
I'm OK.
Really.
My heart is off the coals.
I'm not walking wounded.
I'm not where you left me standing.
There's no blame anymore.
Who knows, maybe someday we'll talk it out over a cherry pie.
But I have a feeling someday will never find us.
That's all I have to say.

You don't need to call me back.

I'm the green light on your answer machine.
Hoping you'll press play.

Grass

Sarah Jane Justice

I tend a churning sea of yellow-green
A tide that ebbs and flows with droning buzz
Sea-shell blossoms echo worker's hum
Bathed on shores that sprout with algae weeds

I spread my sail in waving Hills Hoist sheets
Set in speed while spinning wild in wind
Emerald grass glints bright in bouncing sun
An ocean built from softly shaded blades

I walk across the memory of waves
Captain of a ship that wouldn't drown

Bequeath Only Tears

George Whitestone

Verdant Earth that mother nature bathed in holy dew,
And breathed in life that reflected all her might.
To show creation led in perfect span and hue.
Man's cupidity has left the goddess in a plight.
Man cry the tears of shame.

Alas, the trees, That sheltered man from wind and snow.
Took in his breath and made it pure again.
When they are gone where do the birds and beings go.
No more, their simple, safe domain.
Oh cry the tears of shame.

Rue the water, tainted, turned and spoiled.
Though once of value, held in high esteem,
Now plastic motes in oceans, living creatures soiled.
While underground in search of gas, polluted waters stream.
Man these are the tears of shame.

Despair the air, where once the winged creatures flew.
Up there, that once was pure and clean.
Down there below, where all the species leapt and ran and grew,
Man tainted with his acts so mean.
Oh cry the final tears of shame.

Black Thumb

Amelia Clare Wright

When I was young,
my mom used to tell me she had a
black
thumb
because she killed every plant she touched.

"I can't grow a thing"
except a
child in your
womb,
I wanted to tell her.

I have a bamboo plant
named Darla.
She sits in a clear glass
with nothing but water and sunlight
to vivify her.

Darla was given to me because she never complains,
just grows taller and
shares new leaves with me every so often,
thanking me for keeping her
roots drenched.

Keys ivory and black.
My mother's voice whole and rich like
fudge or heavy cream, filling me up.
Mine young, rosy: crystal or skipping stones.
Together something born from oneness.

She helped me find the harmonies,
taught me where my breath should be,
showed me my notes on the piano.
Her smile while I sang
budded me.

I have a money tree
named Sprout.
He sits in a white pot
with five miniature tree trunks
intertwining.

Sprout has seventy-six broad and
light green leaves,
which is twenty-six
more
than when I bought him four weeks ago.

My mother on the cherry hardwood floor with me
telling me secrets about
pasts and fear that
sound like
truth and funhouse mirrors.

She is eight inches
shorter than I,
but I am always
looking up
at her.

I have a pink succulent
named Penelope.
When I dig my fingernail
into her leaves,
they squirt her jelly insides at me.

Penelope has lived through
floods and droughts
and limbs broken.
She thrives through strife
like anyone wishes they could.

Three years old,
a temper tantrum:
Gasping
Breaths
And
Sobs.

My mom holding me in her arms,
and it turned out
all I needed was
someone to remind me that I was
loved.

I named my ivy
Erin,
after my mom.
The most breathtaking
green leaves with white stripes.

After a week, her leaves
withered and
cracked and
fell to the soil beneath her.
Her branches sagged.

She was like she might die,
like I might, too,
have a
black
thumb.

But that was before
I filled her soil, with
the water of
the lifeforce she gave to me,
and grew her up again
to buoyant vines—
tall and straight spine,
belonging and bloodline.

street view

Lucy Tyrrell

for only a second at driving speed
white letters on the green pasture
of a sign announce two towns—
Buffalo—with arrow straight ahead
Bison—with arrow to the right
and whatever you call them
not one in sight

months later, I wish I had stopped
taken a photograph
of the intersection, the sign
now too far away to return
any time soon

wait—I can
search Google maps
find Spearfish, head north
toward Medora
revisit the same highway

I finger-haul the amber figure
with the red bandana
onto Route 85 rolling north—
this two-lane that crosses
grass and sage

double yellow line
straight as an arrow
advances between rumble strips
edging the cracked-asphalt shoulder

wires dip between poles
send voices and light
to somewhere over the rise
barbed wire hems in
the once-boundless plains
except for the sky shuffle
of white clouds

I click forward past occasional
flat beds and a white truck
just beyond the first turn
to the closed weigh station
there's the sign—
green with white arrows
for the two towns

once they ambled
the undulating green by the millions
roamed in thick robes
breathed warm fog into the blizzard
killed by arrows for sustenance

now they're a white-lettered exhale—
a blur in the rear-view mirror
a green sign
and whatever you call them
not one in sight

At the grove

Piet Nieuwland

In the grove of luminary beings /
      happy in the patterns of trees
Canopies surprise us /
      with their lush foliage of emerald stars
Amongst silken tents of wind /
      the first trembling gossamer on the silvery mirror
The landscape of your iris dissolves /
      into subtle glints of kapowairua
In this sanctum of luxuriant shade /
      cool damp and ferny silence
The eyes of every creature gaze /
      on a vault of the past
Clouds ferment on the Parihaka skyline /
      tanekaha sway to the cries of children

The Verdancy of Green

Ruth Sabath Rosenthal

Green, being my favorite color, I chose
an emerald satin gown for my junior prom.
(Its chartreuse sequins down the side seams
& around the neck & hem had it screaming
out from its rack!)

Just on the cusp of the dating scene & not
knowing any teenagers outside of school,
I asked a home-room guy, named Gene,
to be my date. Gene seemed an ok choice,
but by the end of the evening, he screamed
of boredom; so when he tried to kiss me

good night, in lieu of saying something mean,
I sneezed, apologized, then yelled *good night;*
that was the last I'd seen of Gene, till running
into him 13 years later. What a real good looker
he turned out to be! To my surprise, Gene beamed

upon seeing me. Maybe it was the green blouse
I wore that lifted him out of a funk; or maybe
he dreamed of bumping into me one day, though long-
leaning on the side of caution for fear of another
rejection. Who knows? & who'd ever think I'd be
keenly interested in Gene, & he'd have the self-
esteem enough to hazard asking me out? Believe it

or not, I got a friend's dream-team makeup artist
& hair-dresser to doll me up for the date. Not only
was Gene easy on the eyes, I found him interesting,
too; plus, he had a dream job, & it didn't hurt that
he seemed to have lots of green in the bank. So,
I agreed to a 2nd date &, by the 6th, we weren't
just "seeing" each other, if you get what I mean!

One Halloween, 15 months later, we dressed up
as Queens — me, regal with rhinestone tiara &
emerald velvet cloak, he, in full drag. What a lark!
We were voted Queens of the night by a bunch
of drunks (Jim Beam, the party-drink of choice that night).

By then, being inseparable, we got engaged &
moved into a dream condo overlooking the 18th hole
of the greenest golf course I'd ever seen. Green still
very much my favorite color, one day last week,
while Gene was out putting, in between a tedious job-
related task, I *Googled* "Green" & here is what
appeared on my computer screen:

Green *symbolizes:* ***dark green*** *represents greed, ambition, and wealth;* ***yellow-green*** *stands for sickness, jealousy, and cowardice;* ***olive green*** *represents the traditional color of peace.*

Green *is obtained by mixing Yellow (trials) with Blue (Word of God). Therefore, the biblical meaning of color* ***green*** *is* immortality. *(The leaf shall not wither (psa 1:3)*

Green *is also symbolic of resurrection which we see each Spring.*

Green *has a number of traditional associations in Islam: In the Quran, it is associated with paradise. In the 12th century,* ***green*** *was chosen as dynastic color by the (Shiite) Fatimids. After the Fatimid dynastic color,* ***green*** *remains particularly popular in Shi'ite iconography, but it is also widely used by Sunni states, notably in the flag of Saudi Arabia*

An Ancient River

Mark Tulin

An elderly woman lives in a corner duplex,
surrounded by untrimmed green hedges.
An easterly breeze occasionally blows
from an ancient river.

In the spring, she plants tomatoes,
patiently waiting for them to ripen,
picking each gently from the stem,
and cradles a half-dozen in her apron.

In the summer, she sits on a folding chair
with her legs dipped in a kiddie pool,
a pool of motherhood
where the waves of painful memories
ebb and flow.

She imagines her son as a boy,
splashing in the shallow water,
sailing his wind-up motorboat,
his eyes green and hair a light brown,
his youthful skin glistening from the sun.

As she dips her toes into the freshwater,
under a little beach umbrella,
she gives a sad smile.
A lifetime of raising a stillborn child
few people would ever know.

Climate Change Fears

Gerard Sarnat

Used to be pale Hollywood folk
worried about Them
coming from Compton to riot

but now, no question, liberal rich peeps
in Malibu seem more scared
of fire's black smoke then flooding

plus consequences of indigenous farmers
giving their newly-elected Trumpian Prez
Bolsonaro a signal that they are open

for business by arsoning Amazonian
green rainforests to create opportunities
for development to make Brazil Great Again.

Growth

Jan Chronister

The county loads shoulders
of our road with gravel,
small gray chips crushed
from the oldest rock in the world.

Six weeks later
weeds grow up through the weight—
amaranth, foxtail, bright yellow
butter and eggs—
anchored by roots
branched in darkness.

Green and healthy,
they remind me
I will push through
tests and diagnosis
into the sun again.

Uaine

Christian Garduno

Spreading thick rope nets
tuned into Radio Cairo
and if you were you and I was me
this would be a different story indeed
She began with eyes of green
they turned witch hazel somewhere in between
don't cut the root when all you need is to cull the leaves
And the rain pitter-patters knowing nothing actually matters

The dead were on fire and the angels lost their damned minds
stardust turns to rust and fate is often fatal
prepare the elephants for battle –
NATO helicopters swirling overhead
as an ancient tune plays on two strings beneath the apricot trees
across these high plains, you are suing me for peace
together we slither back down the coast
into another Qattara Depression

When We Were On the Sea

William Butler

Men wept at their first sight of land,
wept not because they were tired of the sea
but because the land was so green
as to defy their belief so long had they been
farming the ocean.
Grizzled deck hands, their fingers gnarled
from hard work aboard,
torn by windlass and chain, hemp and salt,
on their knees with eyes covered
believed they had been drowned and
were now in Heaven so green was the land.
At last the captain, noting the discomfort
fell off to a starboard tack
sailing further South by Southwest
avoiding any further landfall
until their harvesting be done.
Only then would he turn back,
his course North by Northeast
until he once again made landfall,
and it was winter with snow upon the land
so as not to frighten the crew.
And there they became farmers.

Margaret's Green Man

Laurie Byro

In Memory of my grandmother
Margaret Hollenbeck Haffner
November 19, 1896–January 11, 1973

In summer, the stream slows enough
for the nimble to wade. River rocks
create a path for dragonflies
and damsels to rest.
Chalky blue with crazy neon eyes,
we watch them flit and hover, too
exhausted to mate.

Their eyes are like berries the Green Man
favors. You, who won't believe,
smile when I speak of his visitations.
December, he trails me, inevitably
seduces the part of me
that still believes in demons.

Watching these creatures,
I think of my mother's mother, Margaret.
It would be simple to say nothing,
to reach for your hand.
"Listen," I say, while they fly in closer
to hear. "Margaret had six children
and seven more pregnancies.
She used coat hangers."

You lift me up, move me into sunlight.
A hummingbird lands
on a doily of Queen Anne's Lace.
"He held a gun under her breast
those nights she didn't want to.
He was a cop."
You shudder, ask me
why I am spoiling our walk, why
the Green Man must have his way.

"It's the dragons," I say,
as they chase each other, flashing red.
"She told us as kids, they could
darn our lips shut if we dared
tell on them."

My hand covers my mouth.

Give Me the Herbivores in Life

Larry Lefkowitz

Give me the herbivores in life.
The gentle browsers, the gentle tempered.
Each nibbling at his own grass.
How unlike the carnivores
running after prey, seeking fangs,
bringing threat and fear into
the world. The placid cud chewer
eschews becoming Machiavelli. The meat-eater
covets it. The herbivore writes memoirs,
the carnivore, "How I Became a Success."
The greening of the world
awaits.

Weeds

Chelsea Logan

The world outside the house is wild, the front yard
sprinkled with weeds that might be flowers
to eyes that need a respite from too much
looking inward. Tiny violets must be prettier

than grass. I might buy them in a grocery store,
impress the people there who made lists,
buy food in cans. I'd harness the natural world
beneath the ceiling tiles, a connoisseur

with a shopping cart. But this is an excess,
a dizziness I can't afford. These flowers, I'm told,
are undesirable – indiscriminate, too small
for a vase. So I pay men to cut the color

from the yard. They conquer the flowers,
leaving behind a docile sea of green
and for a moment, it feels easy. It feels
like maybe this is what I wanted all along.

The Last Olive

Michael Berton

the last olive
on the plains in Spain
will not touch
any fork on a plate
of paella
it will be
the last
olive on earth

in front of me
a petite dish
a black and green mix
ten or so pitted

the last olive
will abolish the euro
and shake the world economy
the last olive
will not run
for Prime Minister of Catalonia
nor will it prevent
African immigration
into Europe

popping them
to my mouth
a suck then scrape
with my teeth
the meat from the pit

the last olive
will not partake
in a dry martini
nor baked into
a loaf of peasant bread

just as a woman
in a burgundy slit skirt
traipses by my sidewalk table
with an olive complexion
evident up to the inner thigh

nor will it be
ground into tapenade
served as an appetizer
in the swankiest
taverna in Madrid

the olive pit
cracked an explosion
in two halves
as I grimace
surmising a broken tooth
to my relief only chards
swirling my palette

the last olive will reside
unpicked on high high branch
on a slope near Gaudi's Parc Guell
overlooking an expanse
of the Mediterranean

i never got a view
of her walking away
because I had to
get a napkin
to discard the pits

the last olive
must remain
above nationalities
the fragrance of lovers
a healthy diet
it must soil seed
and prosper anew

The Virtues of Roots

Ann Befola

who gave me unerring knowledge of what exists,
the varieties of plants and the virtues of roots (Wisdom 7:15-22)

When Ligia returns the plant I'd nearly killed,
the fir once brown now fragrant green,
she says, *It needs to be in the ground,*
stretching out her hand to finger cool earth.

In my Vermont yard rimmed with pines miles tall,
my husband and I discuss where it would do best, on the hill,
southeast corner, where water runs and forms
streams and moss, where afternoon sun

rests on its arc to horizon. We take shovel to rock-
encrusted clay, pull out slabs of granite and shale,
marveling how good and right mud feels,
set the tree into its new home, pat back soil.

The curious watching. *Oh, pines,* I raise my arms.
My husband asks, *What are you doing?*
Talking to the trees. – Oh.
Please nurture this Norwegian fir, may it
welcome red hawk and owl, squirrel and vole.
You provide the home, we dug the hole.
And I walk away, a green
beneficence on my back.

Coffee Good Friday Morning

Ed Ruzicka

I sip coffee plucked out of shade
on the side of an Andean mountain
by me, my daughter, and my son-in-law.
We were shown how to whisk the beans
over a splay of fire, a few lit twigs.

With quick wrists we stirred them in a clay pot
worn, parabolic, evenly cast. Roasted them
till the wing of a bird passed its shadow
through the beans. Till the beans gained
the laden aroma I now enjoy in Louisiana

where green leaves wag in spring wind.
Robust branches are what my eyes see
as this rich brew takes me back onto

that mountainside where every muscle ached
after a three day hike over wind-punished passes,
along ledges, under snow-caps. Then down
into mists, dangled orchids, flocks of butterflies
as we picked out steps through roots and muck.

At that coffee farm I could have clicked a photo
of my daughter when she lifted a long bamboo pole
to work the edge of a tiny net tied onto the pole's end
against an avocado stem. Avocado trees grow to
thirty feet there. The avocado gave way, dropped
into the net. She brought it down. Handed the fruit
to a women dressed in heavy mountain garb
who placed the avocado on a ledge in sunlight.

I could have taken that photo but I was too ragged,
too exhausted, too at peace with everything I had
ever done and could not move one single muscle
except to watch two eagles lift into great helixes
of wind that disappeared behind tail feathers.

Greenhorn

Marsha Mittman

Great-grandfather
He went AWOL
From the Tsar's army
Fully knowing if caught
He'd be shot but
Figuring he'd die
Anyway fighting the war
So he took a chance
Escaped in a blizzard
And started walking across
Russia, towards the west,
Always west, to Europe
And any port with a ship
Sailing for fabled America
It took nine long hard years
But he persevered and
Achieved his dream
Arriving in legendary
New York City everyone
Called him a greenhorn,
A derogatory slang term
For an inexperienced immigrant
But to great-grandfather
"Greenhorn" meant freedom
The sweetest word ever

Under Lockdown, Manchester

Mantz Yorke

The side-roads are quiet:
only a few cars
and an occasional empty bus
trundle to the city.

Cherries and magnolias
are firework bursts,
and burgeoning green
has yet to flesh out

the skeletons of limes
or the huge splay of an acer
that once supported
a tree house for the kids.

We notice anew
the whites, the fresh greens,
vivid against the deep blue
of an unpolluted sky.

Rhombus of Brightness

Stephen Wren

Sarah was happy
Watches of the teatime sun
A rhombus of brightness
Changed the lawn's tone
From lime to light lime
Down near St. Margaret's Bay
Ranges of green, palettes
With yellows melted
Into white hot fire
On water seemingly calmed
Photons were bedfellows
Of the balsam firs
They took centre-stage
Silhouetted and tranquil
The green's deep vibrancy
Energised Sarah
Colour transmissions
New varieties of green
Opened to her lenses

New hues, that differed
Olive, shamrock green
Pear green that saturated
Her soul with gentle peace
Populous chromas
Her body lifted
By green's comforting manner
She loved Nova Scotia
And its life of green

Willowspring

Paula Bonnell

Among the dark branches
bare branches
appear highlights: willowdawn
Salix babylonica
showing chartreuse

In a breeze, yellow commotion

Spring is a cold season
lit by willows
The riverpath a willowway
goldgreen tresses

Up close –
the trailing strands
that flow from the branches
are fuzzed and crisscrossed with catkins
like ties on a kite's tail
They are frizzled and yellow
or frizzy and green

From a distance –
they dazzle a little
the pure traces of the downtrailing

Fringes stir in a tremolo, greengold
then in a moment's hesitation
their glow lessens
Green hints become leaves' upholstery
spring's mystery
thickens
to form
the green statuary of summer

The Green Boots

Mark Hudson

I was a kid in the seventies. There was the blizzard of 1979. Or was it another year? There seemed to be a lot more snow in those days, before global warming.

I had a pair of green boots, which I wore to school, in the snowstorm. One day I was waiting for the school bus, and I was standing on top of a giant mountain of snow, as if I was the king of the mountain.

Suddenly, I slipped, and went sliding down the mountain of snow on my green boots. I didn't fall, but it was like I was skiing down the mountain, feet first.

I then went skating into the middle of the icy road, and came to a halt in front of a car that had to slam on the brakes. I could tell he was really pissed. He extended his middle finger, and I could see him uttering profanities out loud in his car.

I went to the side of the road and felt like I was having a heart attack. I thought, I could've got hit by that car! For some reason, I felt my green boots were a good luck charm. I wore my green boots with pride.

At one point, I was in Chicago with a kind of rock and roll teenager looking after me while my parents were with some friends. I guess I was giving her a hard time, because she said, "Don't let me make fun of you, or you'll cry."

I said, "No, I won't!" and then we exchanged insults as if it was a contest.

But then she poked fun at my green boots, and suddenly I thought I was going to cry. Didn't she know those boots saved my life?

I didn't cry though, but I was always somewhat sensitive. And I didn't cry either, when I almost got hit by that car. Different things affected me differently as a child.

But I never forgot the green boots story, and glad it didn't lead me to joining the army.

The Park

Declan Geraghty

The park
Rolling in parts, flat in others
Like carpet when the grass is cut
Where addiction began
Green stains on me jeans and black stains on me soul
Lost in alcoholism for years
And years became seasons and sometimes went by like weeks
What was I looking for in the park
Was I looking to be free of pain or thoughts
Free of challenge and dejection
A temporary release from worry and anxiety
Only for anxiety and worry to come back harder
Accompanied by their friends paranoia and despair
We'll drink away depression, he's not welcome here
And the elements weather our faces along with the drinking
What were once young beautiful hopeful faces
Now contorted and battle scarred, sometimes diseased
It's the park you see
It has that hold on me
It still has
And how much work it took to be idle
How much did it cost to be idle
Everything probably
It cost everything.

An Everglades Romance

Karla Linn Merrifield

As if in a fragile kingdom of patient desire,
Rhizophora mangle shoots downward
from its tangled boughs above:
aerial roots.
Return several years later,
they've reached water at last.
As wished, they have grown longer.
Such is the thirst of the red mangrove,
she sets out on bended knee
her slim-legged prop roots
so as to walk into Florida Bay .
It could take a century
for Land to marry Sea
at the foot of this tree.
According to its sweet destiny, her species
will shed its sacrificial yellow leaves one by one:
salt-laden—her tears, her kisses—
her yearning fulfilled: to be ever verdant.
She is a creature of both ecotones,
a being of shifting edges, of tides and tremors,
reaching slowly, walking slowly toward
invisible boundaries, crossing borders.
O, patient union, it was meant to be;
her kingdom comes:
red-named, yellow-leaved, green-hearted.

What You Put Me Through

John Grey

You are all for the simple dog paddle
or relaxing on this rippling surface
with just the gentlest kicks nudging you forward.
You tell me it's the nearest thing to floating.
So are those fish nibbling at my toes
or nothing but smelly green seaweed feeling me up?
Yes, it is beautiful,
if you don't consider what lurks below.

You reckon your body's so soothed
it's as if the supple fingers of a thousand masseurs
have just been through with it.
I'm trembling.
Could be the cold.
Could be the effort required
just to stay in one place.

You're suspended, you tell me,
the perfect balance of weight and fluid.
I'm a meeting ground for pains in muscles
seldom used,
a restaurant critic in some dive
where everything on the menu is salt.

You imagine you're in love. I see myself
as one more drowning victim,
his useless body ripped to shreds
by the prettiest coral you ever saw

I grab your body,
like only land in sight.
But, based on where I stand with you,
you're really just more ocean.

Green Heaven

Michael Hall

The little park is locked and chained,
behind its railings nature has reclaimed the space.
Its grass uncut, its bushes jungle thick,
the place in which I grew lies lost, forgotten, derelict.
It hurts my heart to see that no-one cares.
When I was young this little park was home to me.
A place to play, a place to dream,
a place to while away those endless summer days;
my own green heaven in a dull grey post-war world.
Then the grass was closely tended, borders neatly groomed,
with flowerbeds bright, packed sardine tight
with cheerful, vibrant blooms.
Around its asphalt paths I reckless rode my bike.
Its screeching brakes and clanging bell, annoying old folks
I could tell, while mothers rocking babies in their prams
would raise their hands and bid me hush
as I sped by with pedals flying fit to bust.
I'd chase grey pigeons, send them flapping to the trees,
then on the swings take flight myself
and glimpse blue sky between my knees.
I'd dip the ponds with string and jar in search of wary fish,
and one time, stretching just too far,
I briefly joined them in their water world,
scrambling frightened back to shore,
still with the string but minus jar.

Sometimes I'd go in search of big game,
creeping stealthy through the bushes, treading gently,
careful not to step on fragile flowers.
Lions and tigers proved elusive – not so startled lovebirds
I found hidden, nestled cosy in their secret, leafy bowers.
In the centre of the park there was a gilded iron bandstand.
Upon its stage I sometimes stood to play my air trombone.
People passing by would stop and watch me
standing proudly, braying loudly, showing off
my home grown, often off-tone, music show.

How happy bright those distant sunshine days.

But now the little park is shackled tight with locks and chains,
and nature, held so long at bay, has stolen back
to claim the place again.
The place I played in, made my home in,
built my dreams in, all so very long ago
is now a ghostly empty home, a twilight zone
where only docks and thistles grow.
My head brims full with questions as I mourn this awful sight.
How could they let this happen?
Someone really needs to put this situation right.
The Town Hall holds the answers,
like they hold those padlock keys.
It's the usual problem – lack of cash,
so all the budgets have been squeezed.
In the end it's down to money,
that's why they've locked these gates.
The answer's simple – close the park – or else put up the rates.

Voice of Autumn

John Davis

And then you were not young
The bend in your step didn't
bend like a river

Your walk in the glen
was an uneven scuffle
on stones, an ashen stroll

Your color was gray, not green
like a stamen but gray
among the evergreens

Woven among the forest trees
and Queen Anne's lace, strips
of sunlight followed you like boogiemen

You listened to moss
There among fallen limbs
you listened to leaves

to lichen and dew light
You were not the tree bark that had chosen
darkness You were the silent amen

You were the oxygen
handwoven every morning
that lengthened each day you woke to

The Palm

Miriam Drori

Imagine an arm held straight up.
High above the cars,
The people, the buildings.
The arm is thin and brown – almost black.
The hand wears a dark green lace glove with a brown cuff.
Its fingers are splayed, its palm turned towards you.
That's me, the palm.

No, no, you misunderstand.
I'm not that sort of palm at all.
I'm a tree, grown so tall
I tower over everything,
Come sun, come rain, come…

I shudder when I think of the winter of twenty thirteen.
White flakes falling on my leaves.
Silently resting on my poor branches,
Pushing them down.
So heavy, so very cold.

You who venture out,
Wrapped in thick boots, warm coat and woolly hat,
Spare a thought for me,
Alone, bare to the elements, vulnerable.
A palm out of heat.

Tunnel of Green

Howard Brown

A two-lane blacktop crawls up
the side of the mountain, twisting
and turning back on itself like a
great, coiling king snake.

The verdant walls of this labyrinth,
randomly adorned by the fragile
blossoms of dogwood, redbud and
Japanese honeysuckle.

Where sunlight manages to breech
the sheltering canopy, it softly dapples
the shadowed surface of the road. So,
on you ride, climbing, ever climbing,

And, finally, reaching the top, the sun
gone now as scattered drops of rain begin
to fall, aslant in the face of a chill, west
wind, storm clouds hover in the distance.

Yet this is not what you'll remember as
you lie in bed that night. Rather it's the
time spent traversing the long tunnel of
green which will pervade your dreams.

Winter Morning

Anna Mioduchowska

The pine green tights I channel up my legs,
over my hips, hoodwink my winter-blanched skin

with the promise of mountain lake, evergreens
skinny-dipping in sun-glazed water, trout, loon.

Venus slippers sprout from my bedroom floor
when I am greened from waist to toe.

Golden fleabane, fireweed and juniper line the stairs
leading me out, the pavement leading me on –

a vision of a nymph accompanied by a chorus
of verdant echoes in the morning rush hour.

All too soon silenced by a run slashing my calf,
the evergreens, the juniper in fast retreat.

I grope my way out of the way, muttering
woe and *woe* at the oncoming traffic,

and *rest-in-peace* at the long lost auntie
bowed over a laddered stocking

webbed over her hand. Good light overhead,
her glasses abandoned for better aim,

she hooks the silky unravelling, rethreads it
one rung at a time. The long lost art

of invisible mending mastered in times
of scarcity. Promises of run-proof hose.

Verdant Envy

Debbie Wiess

Whoever said "the grass is
always greener..." was right.
Since he moved in ten years
ago, my neighbor and I
have lived side by side,
our properties contiguous.
The harmony of the quarter
very soon was disrupted
by an unspoken rivalry
that simmered
and then erupted
like a smoldering spark
in the underbrush of a forest.

For the expanse of terrain
of his domain quickly began
to outshine mine, which had
formerly been so coveted
and the source of envy.
It was inexplicable!
It was dastardly!
How his turf had become
lusher and more verdant,
not a single dandelion nor
other weed daring to poke
its head out to blemish it.

Year after year,
day in and day out,
I observed his activities
in the yard and garden.
Noting his techniques, methods
and the hours dedicated to
tending his lawn and plantings.
He was assiduous, yes, in the
extreme in his ministrations.
But beyond that, I had
not remarked anything
out of the ordinary.
All being essentially
the same as for me.

Nevertheless,
his results were superior.
I remained flabbergasted
and simply fit to be tied.
Oh, yes, the grass was
greener on the other side
of the property line,
that could not be denied.
And the reason for it to this
day leaves me mystified.
The only explanation left
was he must have made
a bargain with the Devil
or there had been some
intervention of the Divine.

Long May Your Big Jib Draw

Shannon Kernaghan

Desperate: I lost my job
need money for the wife and kids for Christmas
$4,500 firm – this mint Kawasaki dirt bike
can be yours!

This bike was my only treat in five years
of being away, sharing rooms with strangers,
strange lands
to send money home.

My well-worn path to prosperity
along with other East Coasters
limited prospects at home
led me to a good job in the oil sands
enough to buy a green-grassed house for family
back east.

Blindsided in a meeting to discuss sales projections
before I could even sit down, my pale manager spoke –
Freddie, this is your last day, I'm sorry, man.
I am now one of the countless, from steel-toed
rig hands to latte sipping executives.

Since oil prices began their dine & dash to a hard crash,
I am one of the upheaval stories
of layoffs pummeling
countless small towns that rely
on the energy sector
now caught in oil's sucking undertow.

Where is the bungee bounce-back?
Why has dread replaced optimism?
Not our first rodeo with a bust
so why no swift recovery in my horoscope?
(The wife calls it *horror-scope*, now that my benefits
are as empty as that cup of latte in that empty office tower.)

Can't lose the green-grassed house back home
need somewhere to live when I surrender here
how long can a buddy keep his chin up
keep the lights on
when I watch repo tows hurtling past
and drawers dumped quickly onto front yards
when I hear words like delayed, cut and dried up
slashed and suicidal
dreams in decline
hope shrivels like my credit score.

$3,900 or best offer, this bike can be yours today!

The tangled garden

Karen Davidson

How long before
MacDonald reached
for his paintbrush,
having waited most of August
for the sunflowers
to tilt their spotlights?
Did he chase off
jays and neighbourhood
children? Did he startle a cat?

Each season
re-arranges palette and canvas:
today the viewer
is held at bay,
like a dun-coloured
dog on a radiant leash.
Either stand to one side
in the gallery

or pace the periphery

where what lies
beyond the feeder blurs;
now rogue sunflowers
lose sway
to a rain forest
of bougainvillia
and what I long to be
hothouse orchids,
lime green and clingy.

It's winter out there.

I've stepped in to find my toad.

* After visiting J.E.H. MacDonald's The Tangled Garden at the
National Gallery in Ottawa, in January 2020.

Pan Flash

Guy Chambers

    clayey gray
    clairvoyant slant

    cast stones at feet
    from the newspaper stand

picture green, blue
one point of view

    pan flash
    moment fame

    mankind
      colorblind
        mind

finger pointed
one eye fence line

    ink
    filled with
    lost shadow

    vast past
    absurd millions of darkness
    downright hindsight

imagery gallery
treachery scenery
spidery thievery

        digest novel
        misread

        jest noel
        miss render

chest nickel
flipping in the air

        embezzle thoughts
        to the beanstalk talk

    world walks this way
others stop and think

        eyes staring back
        reason the same

    what after this

How Aussie is that

Dave Clark

On a lush, pine green golf course
near Semaphore beach,
the sun cashes in
as the feather clouds go on strike

And I catch a momentary glimpse
of a man in motion,
with skin as smooth
as cacti
and the colour of undercooked chicken

A thick saltbush tree blocks him from view;
I tell my brother that in three glorious seconds
he needs to look over his shoulder

He counts down, then turns
to survey a doyen
pedalling at pedestrian pace,
wearing only a faded yellow helmet
and black jocks

How Aussie is that, we exclaim,
prioritising safety
over shorts

Birdbrain

Paula Rudnick

The ancients used to stretch their ear lobes
to make room for decoration.
We humans love embellishment.
By three we understand that unadorned,
we are not good enough.
Scientists say that parrots
have the IQ of a human toddler.
They can speak in complete sentences
and know the difference between red and green.
Parrots reach their half-life around forty,
still aware that red and green are not the same,
still squawking for a cracker,
while humans have learned to mix flour with water,
set the oven to 350 and voila.
Captive parrots lose their minds when tethered
to an indoor perch for prolonged intervals.
They peck at anklets, scream and sway,
pluck out feathers till they cannot fly,
the only edge they have over us humans
besides knowledge at age three
that baubles on distended earlobes
are no substitute for self-esteem.

St Patrick's Day

Colleen Moyne

You thought you looked so handsome
In that green shirt
with the white collar and cuffs,
once so hip in the seventies
but now a rare breed indeed.

It hung in your closet all year,
suspended in time,
waiting for that one day –
when from every Irish household
green shirts emerged
like butterflies from closet cocoons,
shaken out, pressed crisp
and paraded down at Paddy's pub

a perfect match to the dubious brew
of green-tinted beer,
guzzled down gullets
in copious amounts
as lubrication for wailing strains
of Danny Boy and Galway Girl

Drunken toasts to the home country,
old jokes and sentimental tears,
a wobbly walk home
and that green shirt would be packed away
along with the memories
for yet another year.

Finding green
Mary Trafford

What is green?
Does it have a name?
I search among paint tubes,
colour swatches.
Green eludes me, the words that
capture and describe that
particular moment: green.
But I can feel it.

Green is when the aching stops,
smooth green relief easing me
into movement: fluid, free,
going where I will, unimpeded, sure.
I want that green, to slather on joints,
go deep:
eucalyptus, spearmint. Comfort.

Green is knowing, to await
the veil of tears back of the eyes,
knowing it will come,
in its own slow way, sweet yet bitter,
knowing I can wait:
scallions, lemon balm. Sorrow.

Finding green is my mission.
It is my calling,
it beckons me down
a forested trail:
recognition marks the way.

Of ringbarked trees by moonlight

Ron Wilkins

Each time I pass at night
the island in its rippled sea—a furrowed field,
   I see bare trunks and limbs so touched
and silvered by the moon they must be precious.
Not long ago the trees gave shade to cattle
   but the pasture fallen now to the relentless march
of wheat, they must yield their long-established ground.

   Yet somehow, like soldiers fallen in a foreign field
they gain in stature by their death.
   Could we then spare a thought for myriad trees
that gave their lives to make ours more abundant,
   the warming fires, the comforts of furniture,
even humble fence posts to define our lands?
   Also those, that sleeping side by side
support our trains and journeys through the land,
   and as telegraph poles, standing to attention,
shouldering the vital burden of communications.

Were each tree possessed not only of a botanical,
but an individual name, inscribed when dead,
   their service noted on a memorial wall, this wall
would snake around our States and Territories.
   My proposal is absurd? I understand.
Yet marshalled in the park the eucalypts are straight,
   and tall, and dressed in green – so soldierly.

Perfect

Fiona M. Jones

I saw a lawn
of perfect green
in single shade
unfadeable
Unsown, ungrown
but edge to edge
a carpet kept
as tidy and correct
as someone else's
paradise
that I believe is
sin
Where nothing dies
but nothing lives
and nothing dares
disturb the sterile stasis
of the scene
A turf that's
not of earth
and less than garden

It's easy-care
and always there
convenient to keep
No weed or mess
or leaves or moss
No butterflies or bees
Just bristle-textured
Baize.

Cooking in the glut

Robyn Lance

Sprawled across the bench, this morning's harvest
waits for me, a mumma with no mojo:
zucchinis, long and sleek, darkest blackjack green
or lightly flecked with white, bulging at one end
but caught, lying doggo under their leaf, before
they could morph to stuffed marrow size.

Aubergines, baby-skin smooth in un-dimpled purple
– monarchs of the beds. Tomatoes, red
ladies in waiting, plump and begging to be bitten.
Bumpy young carrots with rats' tails
so orange you could call 'em blue.
They await their final destiny, for me
to cut, spice, blend and cook but this
mojoless mumma's got her head in a book.

A Prickly Relationship

David Atkinson

For long periods you seem aloof,
you make no effort.

I spend so much time waiting for you,
checking on you at all hours

even at night. Our affinity appears
strained; I keep hoping you will

display your better side. There is always
a great sense of drama about you

yet you remain erect, unbending,
inflexible. Rarely, it occurs perhaps

once a year, you make a grand entrance,
laughing and preening in the middle

of the night, ostentatious and spectacular,
floral and fragrant; at last your beauty

ensures my persistence has been worthwhile.
And yet by dawn, like Cinderella

fleeing the ball, your bloom has wilted.
Queen of the night cactus.

The Way of the Grasshopper

Luciana Croci

an embroidered patch sewn on a denim jacket
a grasshopper inside a *tao* circle
when you were 12
wore your heart on your sleeve
a grasshopper unlikely hero
weak but nimble tiny but brave
manoeuvring between good and evil
hopping a straight line
from himself to himself

then you reached your teens
shed your boyhood skin and boyhood dreams
no place for a puny insect
among testosterone-boisterous boys
mind says declutter add to Vinnie's bag,
heart says I cannot part
with these skinny lines of green
stitched between white and black
cannot discard what you,
my son, once found

I've found the green

Jill Vance

Tea Olive
Pink Dogwood
Flowering Peach
Crab Apple
Magnolia
Juniper
Pampas
Yellow Jasmine
Carolina Cherry
Camellia
Amen Corner
White Dogwood
Golden Bell
Azalea
Chinese Fir
Firethorn
Redbud
Nandina
Holly
and
the nineteenth hole
at Augusta National

Poppies

Jan Haag

I scattered the seeds last year alongside the driveway
in a long-neglected strip bordering my neighbor's property,
the garden goddess in her floppy hat, dirt-colored gloves,
who nowadays crouches in her backyard, picking weeds
as if they were delicate flowers. "To make sure I get 'em all,"
she tells me, spending hours clearing a sizeable patch.

She persuaded me to remove the small fence
dividing us, and, after I reluctantly agreed, when her
husband didn't get to it, she took sledgehammer
in hand and bashed down the old redwood.
But because its timbers remained cemented in place,
she left the old gate, a lone sentinel of former separation.

Then the garden goddess dove into the fragment
of undivided dirt, digging up packed clay, adding
amendments to fluff it up. She'd work a fraction, then
I'd upend another, later she'd return, until it became
a little patch of tilled urbanity, ready for renewal.

Into it she transplanted velvety purple pansies and
lime green sprigs of crawling groundcover,
its leaves the size of a baby's fingernails. I found
a jar of jumbled wildflower seeds in my garage,
a miscellany of hope that I sprinkled with my usual
more-is-better philosophy, dreaming of what might
find its way through the dark and arise—poppies,
blue dicks, wild radish, lupine.

The garden goddess, wielding her cobra-thick hose
and giant nozzle, watered daily, sometimes twice,
turning her devotion to the baby plants.
And, although I had tried and failed for years
to turn this patch of earth into something lovely,
under her daily blessings of artificial rain,
flowers flourished.

Just as the isolation order came down,
the poppies raised their brilliant heads in unison
above lacy greenery, a wildflower choir unfurling
by day to sing praises to the sun and putting
themselves to bed all tucked in at night.

This spring I have contributed nothing to that bit of earth.
It has resurrected itself, prettier than last year.
The garden goddess has added miniature ceramic houses,
an arched bridge and gnomes, small, bearded
fellows with merry smiles. She showers them daily.

Yesterday, as I took out the garbage, I paused to
breathe it all in—happy poppies, storybook houses—
and noticed the gnomes knocked over, perhaps by
the force of the hose, perhaps by cats or by life.
It is easy to get flattened these days, so I crouched
by the poppies, a smile dawning, and set
the little fellows upright again.

It is what we do, day after day now, for each other.
For ourselves.

Plague of locusts

Myrna Garanis

I lead the charge, wielding the thinning kitchen broom,
whacking a path through cankerworms. My mother's
hair protected by a Wheat Pool ballcap, mine with a
borrowed Arctic Cat.

Green bodies cling to the eaves, spin and multiply,
webs barely visible in the morning cool. Hordes
surge up the trunks of century old maples.
We pull down our sleeves, concoct multiple
forms of death.

Beer traps for slugs, plentiful as peas this plague-
filled year. A summer ago it was wasps. If this
blight persists, claims our pundit neighbour,
the lofty maples, already hollowed, will succumb.

My mother and I wrench storm windows from
rotted frames, search for matching screens, a chore
my father used to love. Full steam to palliative care
through an arch of hanging horrors.

My father complains about the soup, barely dents
the bed sheets, his body a weak defence against
invasion. Defying hospital rules, we've packed
a slice of lemon pie for him. Whipped peaks of
of meringue tower high, anything to ease his fall.

In the Next Galaxy

Laura Jan Shore

after Ruth Stone

No one is looking at
their phones.
Technology is obsolete.
Children are schooled
in mental telepathy.
They beam the green laser
of their attention and listen
to the trees grow.
Trees:
their primary tutors.
Whales: their worship.
Back here, we float
on top of our debris, gadgets
lashed together with fishing line.
While in the next galaxy,
they sigh contented, at home
in their fourth dimensional cottages
which none of us can see.

Training Wheels

Shawn Aveningo-Sanders

The old adage
rattled in her head,
her friend's words
of supposed comfort,
Don't worry;
It's just like riding a bike.

But the last bicycle
she remembered riding
had streamers on the handlebars,
clickity-clack straws on the spokes,
and a hot pink banana seat.

One more look in the mirror,
before stepping out
onto the playing field,
which now didn't seem quite so green.
She wished for
a pair of training wheels…

… and a padded push up bra.

Hair

Luke McDonough

When I met you sprigs of green
Budded from your head like
A mistake.

The night was drunk
And I approached you
Like a magnet, Somehow
I was pushed to you.
I cannot remember the impulse.

A month later,
You told me that impressed you,
As if I was the type of person to greet
Strangers at a bar.

I don't know who that was.
I've morphed through so many
Objects, my atoms
Constantly shifting and reorganizing
Into unrecognizable collages.

Old photographs revealed
Blue-green beauty on your head.
All I knew was a faded moss.
You wore a hat
To cover the purgatory.

But in bed I rummaged
Through your skull
Thick, dead cells shared with me.

Your black hair will grow back
Soft and natural like a person
Unscathed.

Black like it always existed,
Like no versions of you
Were harmed in the Interim, like
An Empty chalkboard.

My own a sort of blondish,
Maybe brown maybe
You decide and let me know.

Since youth I have been told
That sunlight rose upon my head
But when I look in the mirror
Dirt rises.

As if I cannot comprehend
This vessel I have been given.

A photo in my phone
Of the last time I saw you.
The light leaks a halo
That perfectly encapsulates you.
Perfectly situated light or
A divine sleight of hand.

A memoriam of your body
As it was once replicated;
Still dirtied with my touch.

Cutting the grass

Melissa Wong

I am outnumbered by the grass that conquered the plains
Yet I have you and together we are our army of two
With the old lawn mower, we shall be unstoppable!

Crawling out of the dirt to stand with the flowers
I stand above them as I dig my painted toenails in the soil
And I stand firm as I plug in the electric lawn mower

The lawn mower groans as you try to push it forward
The half-dead machine screams in pain and dies
You arch your plucked eyebrow as I rant at the sunrise

We watch golden light cut through the clouds like a rainbow
Its light filtered through white clouds tainted with pink hues
And splashes of tinted light waving in the clouds like a flag

It crowned the thin green grass of the wide fields
Like an ocean of uniform green flora for us to bathe in
We can cut the smug green lawn tomorrow or the day after

Right now, I love you like I love the sky and the earth combined
For you exist in and above all contradictions in my heart
And you promised to go shopping for a new lawn mower later

Vine – The *Big Island* of Hawaii

John Laue

An indigestion of greenness!
       Picasso – after a forest walk

Suddenly I entered a strange landscape
as if all that lived and breathed
had been covered by green camouflage nets.

At first it seemed a welcome change,
the foreground filled with fanciful shapes,
some like castles or cathedrals,

others exotic animals and birds,
all clothed in neat, five-pointed leaves
with small white flowers interspersed.

I stopped a passerby and asked, *What's that?*
Banana poka, he replied, *an introduced species
also known as inch-a-minute vine.*

it's quite handsome, as you can see;
Someone probably imported it as a houseplant,
but then it ran wild – and now this!.

I thought of the trees, some 70 feet tall,
eclipsed by this swift spreading blanket.
Did what appeared to be cute topiary

really disguise a thousand struggles for life?
A score of hungry tendrils wrapped
each tentative bud and branch

tight as gloves on hands
or hangmen's hoods on heads.
If they were removed I believe we'd find

neither leaves nor blossoms, nuts or fruits,
only naked skeletons across these acres
cut off from sun by dominating green.

Fallen Companion

Mary Daurio

The hummingbirds come to the feeder
From the spruce there is no cedar

They land on the clothesline and wait their turn
Occasionally one is impatient, and a war will he earn

Like little men in colorful green and red tuxedos
Bedecked and bejeweled fast as torpedoes

If the feeder is empty on a day
They hover around—feed me they say

One summer morn a sound I heard
The door had opened and hit a tiny bird

His little heart drummed frail
Resuscitation was to no avail

I gently buried him down along the trail
Still through the air his companions sail

I feel the sadness that touched me on that day
Still smile when hovering around—feed me they say

Sans Color

Kathryn Paulsen

That particular green
in high school and maybe elsewhere
that year—the in color for clothes—
wasn't avocado, or chartreuse,

wasn't Kelly green, grass green, pine green, leaf green, sea
green, pea green, olive green, grape green, kiwi green, lime
green, acid green, electric green, bean green, artichoke green,
lettuce green—though lettuce, perhaps, came close.

So it became known as no-color green,
a name special-seeming, oddly pleasing,
though the shade it named
was not flattering to most.

How we embraced the idea
of no color being the
best color—transcending
the idea of colors needing names—

an idea that played
such a large part
in our daily lives—
labeling, dividing, depriving—
consigning to separate worlds.

Weeds in the Wasteland

Joseph Allison

Through the gap in the pavement,
Through the concrete crack,
Through the wastelands, left alone,
We'll grow up strong,
Put down roots and slowly make our home.

We'll split your rock and wasted brick.
We'll reach deep down unseen,
And scab that gash with rain and light,
Our bursts of verdant green.

Flecks of flowers,
Cat's ear, bittercress, thistle,
Shoot up, wild and free.
Buildings to bones, all will be ours!
Give it time.
You'll see.

The Absence of Green, Spring 2020

Deborah Meltvedt

Sipping margaritas, we watch
the tree throw limbs. Femurs
of wood split and green fingers
snap as I wonder if it was
too much Triple sec or Lime juice.
We are on batch #7, one through six
a graveyard in refrigerator shelves.
The slender branches fat with leaves
fall across cars and gutters
littering our lawn without wind
or storm. *Is it the drought?*
Old age? Root rot?
With aching necks and slack bodies
we ask *how did things get this bad?*
and go inside, mix up number eight,
add salt, and hope in failure we
can imagine bringing back a
canopy of hope.

Green Eyes

Kathryn Sadakierski

Envious of my sister's deep blue eyes,
I thought the genetic lottery had been unkind.
In the mirror, the lenses through which I see
Seemed dull in their hue of muddy green.
My mom's birthstone, an April diamond,
Is, of course, a girl's best friend,
While my month of May
Has not diamonds, but an emerald for a gem.

A Gemini, the twins are my sign,
And they can never make up their minds,
So, naturally, I am always
Delving into every book,
Learning new things,
Wanting to forge new paths across many disciplines,
Never limiting myself
To one way of thinking,
Always green,
Striving to know, to see.

Hence, it seems I am surrounded
By all things green,
A shade that perhaps is not an unlucky fate.
At the heart of the hue is a golden light,
Radiant and bold,
Promising and full of life.
Spring is painted green with rebirth,
Green is beautiful in enrobing new earth,
Complementing the blue of the sky;
Without seeing green,
As in the style of Oz's citizens of Emerald City,
Where would we be?
Not seeing the full picture,
Lacking clarity.

Outside Her Window

Dev Berger

Outside my mother's
hospital window
is a sea of green grass gleaming
across the meadows,
whose warmth and
calm she cannot
see nor touch.
She hears my tapping
on the glass, and sees
me holding flesh from my flesh
born at home
and now
held high for
her first look.
She is a fragile vessel
with enough strength
to blow one kiss
that streams through
glass and flies
high above the sea
of verdant waves carrying
my mother's kiss upward,

while serenaded with songs
by field mice.
The kiss is now a
blinding light
piercing three generations,
connecting them with words unspoken
from a kiss that feeds
their hungry hearts
before fading into
a blazing viridescent
stratosphere.

Picture This

Linda Simone

Along the asphalt track
(so many cracks like cobblestone)
I circle sap green nucleus of grass.
Starlings spring
like May flowers in sepia and gray.
Next time, I'll bring some biscuit crumbs.

A denim'd teen hunkers by track's edge,
knees to chin. She hides a grizzled dog
in fortress of her calves. Both
dejected, I strain to see
if the canine has all his legs.

An egret streaks in stark white chalk.
Above, the silhouetted hawk glides
like tip of my poised brush.
Shaggy sheep-clouds mill
about cerulean fields.

Through silver chain link,
baseball diamond glows—
a burnt sienna rivaling the sun.
What color is the breeze?
It sweeps a sheaf
of maple leaves like tumbleweed,
ripples golden crowns of trees.

Off track, soft mottled olive sod
is spongy as my cotton page
that waits at home for buttery paint.

Such lustrous hues!
My flawless morning shadow
keeps its shaded pace,
voiceless, so I absorb and translate.
As my walk ends,
the girl and dog diffuse
like pigment into water.
He has four legs.

A Matter of Substance

Alex Robertson

The magic of television
Now transferred to PC screens
    and phones in this modern age
Something more shown in the final cut
But jiggery-pokery in the 'studio'
A back drop cloak of invisibility
As if possessing superhuman powers
Stage curtains now never used
This 'green screen' is Joseph's dream coat
Providing a plethora of scenes
Stories in themselves
To support the foreground content

A reminder in the briefing notes
Don't wear shades of lime
Unless you want to disappear
        Into the background
Being at one with nature
Is the antithesis of this technology
Stage directions going on in verdant surroundings
An illusionist's toolbox
To set a scene or reinforce the script
Nothing seen of 'blacked out' assistants
Providing a course of action with props
Flying saucers or imagined dragons
Standing out in front of this invisibility
Tricks with the eyes
Found in this visual spectacle
A *trompe*-l'œil of television's backdrop

Remarks in a Writing Studio

Joanie DiMartino

in the style of a whaleship logbook

Wednesday, 20th May 2020
     Com'cd with haiku, some writer's meditations, took in 2 rough drafts of poems. Mid-day employed in revisions, perusing contemporary collections, sundry emails and small tasks to submit manuscript. Latter part attended a reading, sighted another poet, gammed over   green tea. Traded texts. Jotted notes for next volume.   Steady rains. So ends this day.

About Truth Serum Press

Established in 2014, Truth Serum Press is based in Adelaide, Australia, but publishes writers from all parts of the English-speaking world.

Like sister presses Pure Slush Books and Everytime Press, Truth Serum Press is part of the Bequem Publishing collective.

Truth Serum Press formerly published novels, novellas, and short story collections ... but now we only publish smaller, shorter poetry collections ... and, when the mood strikes us, we also publish multi-author anthologies.

We publish in English, and we would gladly publish in other languages if we understood them.

We like stories (and poems) that take us to new places, to new experiences, and inside new minds and hearts.

We also like to laugh.

Visit our website at https://truthserumpress.net/.

Also from TRUTH SERUM PRESS

truthserumpress.net/catalogue

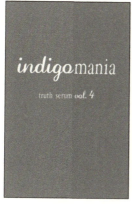 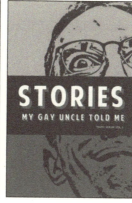 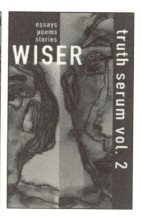

- *Indigomania* Truth Serum Vol. 4
  978-1-925536-03-4 (paperback) 978-1-925536-84-3 (eBook)
- *Stories My Gay Uncle Told Me* Truth Serum Vol. 3
  978-1-925536-86-7 (paperback) 978-1-925536-87-4 (eBook)
- *Wiser* Truth Serum Vol. 2
  978-1-925101-31-7 (paperback) 978-1-925101-32-4 (eBook)

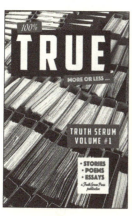 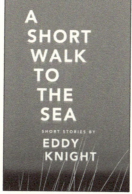 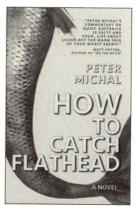

- *True* Truth Serum Vol. 1
  978-1-925101-29-4 (paperback) 978-1-925101-30-0 (eBook)
- *A Short Walk to the Sea* by Eddy Knight
  978-1-925536-01-1 (paperback) 978-1-925536-02-7 (eBook)
- *How to Catch Flathead* by Peter Michal
  978-1-925536-94-2 (paperback) 978-1-925536-95-9 (eBook)

Also from TRUTH SERUM PRESS

truthserumpress.net/catalogue

 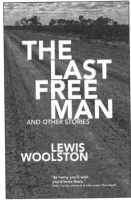 

- *Decennia* by Jan Chronister
  978-1-925536-98-0 (paperback) 978-1-925536-99-7 (eBook)
- *The Last Free Man* by Lewis Woolston
  978-1-925536-88-1 (paperback) 978-1-925536-89-8 (eBook)
- *Filthy Sucre* by Nod Ghosh
  978-1-925536-92-8 (paperback) 978-1-925536-93-5 (eBook)

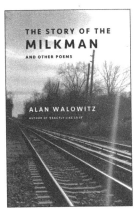  

- *The Story of the Milkman* by Alan Walowitz
  978-1-925536-76-8 (paperback) 978-1-925536-77-5 (eBook)
- *Minotaur and Other Stories* by Salvatore Difalco
  978-1-925536-79-9 (paperback) 978-1-925536-80-5 (eBook)
- *The Book of Acrostics* by John Lambremont, Sr.
  978-1-925536-52-2 (paperback) 978-1-925536-53-9 (eBook)

Also from TRUTH SERUM PRESS

truthserumpress.net/catalogue

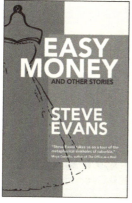  

- *Easy Money* by Steve Evans
  978-1-925536-81-2 (paperback) 978-1-925536-82-9 (eBook)
- *Square Pegs* by Rob Walker
  978-1-925536-62-1 (paperback) 978-1-925536-63-8 (eBook)
- *Cheat Sheets* by Edward O'Dwyer
  978-1-925536-60-7 (paperback) 978-1-925536-61-4 (eBook)

 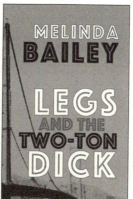 

- *The Crazed Wind* by Nod Ghosh
  978-1-925536-58-4 (paperback) 978-1-925536-59-1 (eBook)
- *Legs and the Two-Ton Dick* by Melinda Bailey
  978-1-925536-37-9 (paperback) 978-1-925536-38-6 (eBook)
- *Dollhouse Masquerade* by Samuel E. Cole
  978-1-925536-43-0 (paperback) 978-1-925536-44-7 (eBook)

Also from TRUTH SERUM PRESS

truthserumpress.net/catalogue

- *Kiss Kiss* by Paul Beckman
  978-1-925536-21-8 (paperback) 978-1-925536-22-5 (eBook)
- *Inklings* by Irene Buckler
  978-1-925536-41-6 (paperback) 978-1-925536-42-3 (eBook)
- *On the Bitch* by Matt Potter
  978-1-925536-45-4 (paperback) 978-1-925536-46-1 (eBook)

- *Too Much of the Wrong Thing* by Claire Hopple
  978-1-925536-33-1 (paperback) 978-1-925536-34-8 (eBook)
- *Track Tales* by Mercedes Webb-Pullman
  978-1-925536-35-5 (paperback) 978-1-925536-36-2 (eBook)
- *Luck and Other Truths* by Richard Mark Glover
  978-1-925101-77-5 (paperback) 978-1-925536-04-1 (eBook)

Also from TRUTH SERUM PRESS

truthserumpress.net/catalogue

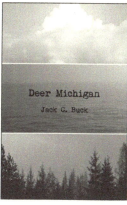
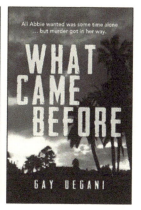

- *Hello Berlin!* by Jason S. Andrews
  978-1-925536-11-9 (paperback) 978-1-925536-12-6 (eBook)
- *Deer Michigan* by Jack C. Buck
  978-1-925536-25-6 (paperback) 978-1-925536-26-3 (eBook)
- *What Came Before* by Gay Degani
  978-1-925536-05-8 (paperback) 978-1-925536-06-5 (eBook)

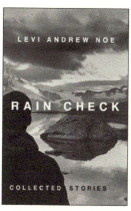

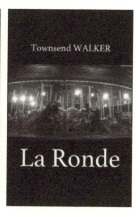

- *Rain Check* by Levi Andrew Noe
  978-1-925536-09-6 (paperback) 978-1-925536-10-2 (eBook)
- *The Miracle of Small Things* by Guilie Castillo Oriard
  978-1-925101-73-7 (paperback) 978-1-925101-74-4 (eBook)
- *La Ronde* by Townsend Walker
  978-1-925101-64-5 (paperback) 978-1-925101-65-2 (eBook)